P

american popular piano

REPERTOIRE

REPERTOIRE

Compositions by
Christopher Norton

Additional Compositions and Arrangements
Dr. Scott McBride Smith

Editor
Dr. Scott McBride Smith

Associate Editor
Clarke MacIntosh

NV Music

Book Design & Engraving
Andrew Jones

Cover Design
Wagner Design

A Note about this Book

Pop music styles can be grouped into three broad categories:

- **lyrical** — pieces with a beautiful singing quality and rich harmonies; usually played at a slow tempo;

- **rhythmic** — more up-tempo pieces, with energetic, catchy rhythms; these often have a driving left hand part;

- **ensemble** — works meant to be played with other musicians, or with backing tracks (or both!); this type of piece requires careful listening and shared energy.

American Popular Piano has been deliberately designed to develop skills in all three areas.

You can integrate the cool, motivating pieces in **American Popular Piano** into your piano studies in several ways.

- pick a piece you like and learn it; when you're done, pick another!

- choose a piece from each category to develop a complete range of skills in your playing;

- polish a particular favorite for your local festival or competition. Works from **American Popular Piano** are featured on the lists of required pieces for many festivals and competitions;

- use the pieces as optional contemporary selections in music examinations;

- Or...just have fun!

Going hand-in-hand with the repertoire in **American Popular Piano** are the innovative **Etudes Albums** and **Skills Books**, designed to enhance each student's musical experience by building technical and aural skills.

- **Technical Etudes** in both Classical and Pop Styles are based on musical ideas and technical challenges drawn from the repertoire. Practice these to improve your chops!

- **Improvisation Etudes** offer an exciting new approach to improvisation that guides students effortlessly into spontaneous creativity. Not only does the user-friendly module structure integrate smoothly into traditional lessons, it opens up a whole new understanding of the repertoire being studied.

- **Skills Books** help students develop key supporting skills in sight-reading, ear-training and technique; presented in complementary study modules that are both practical and effective.

Use all of the elements of **American Popular Piano** together to incorporate a comprehensive course of study into your everyday routine. The carefully thought-out pacing makes learning almost effortless. Making music and real progress has never been so much fun!

Library and Archives Canada Cataloguing in Publication

Norton, Christopher, 1953-

American popular piano [music] : repertoire / compositions by Christopher Norton; additional compositions and arrangements, Scott McBride Smith; editor, Scott McBride Smith ; associate editor, S. Clarke MacIntosh.

To be complete in 11 volumes.
The series is organized in 11 levels, from preparatory to level 10, each including a repertoire album, an etudes album, a skills book, and an instrumental backings compact disc.

ISBN 1-897379-00-5 (preparatory level).--ISBN 1-897379-01-3 (level 1).--ISBN 1-897379-02-1 (level 2).--ISBN 1-897379-03-X (level 3).--ISBN 1-897379-04-8 (level 4).--ISBN 1-897379-05-6 (level 5)

1. Piano music--Teaching pieces. I. Smith, Scott McBride II. MacIntosh, S. Clarke, 1959- III. Title.

MT242.N883A52 2006   786.2   C2006-906213-7

LEVEL P REPERTOIRE

Table of Contents

Skating

WALTZ

Listen closely and make sure
each note has beautiful tone.

Christopher Norton

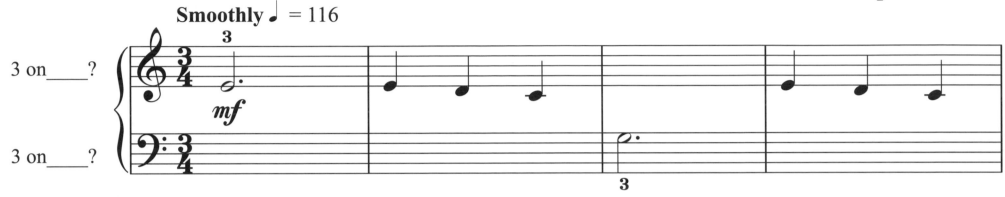

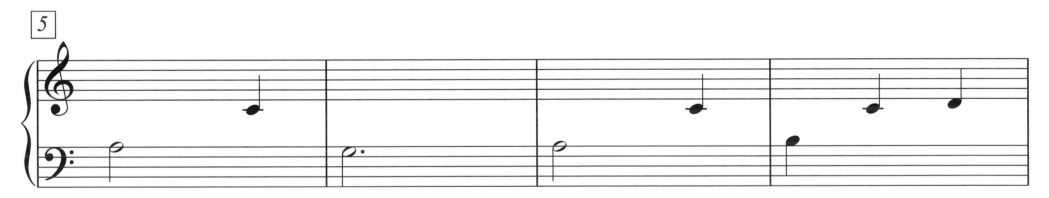

Teacher Duet (student plays one octave higher)

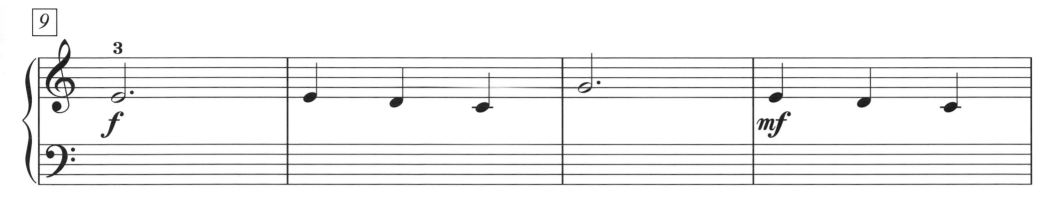

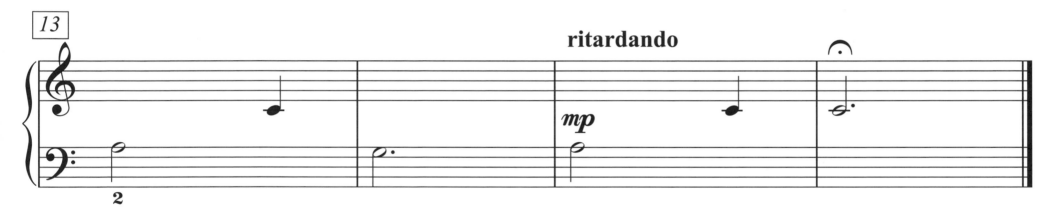

Detection Question: Compare mm. 1-6 with mm. 9-14. Are all the notes the same? If not, which ones are different?

4

Out At Night

SOUL

Make sure that the repeated notes
are light and energetic.

Christopher Norton

3 on____?

3 on____?

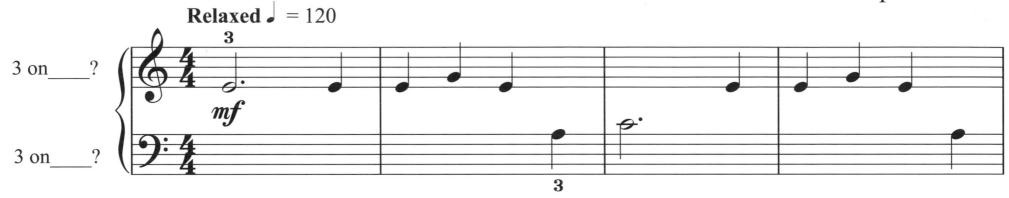

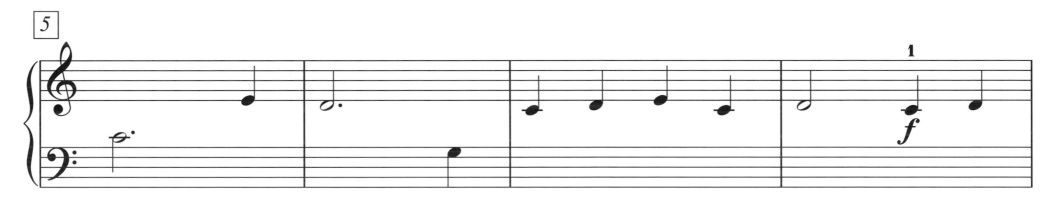

Teacher Duet (student plays one octave higher)

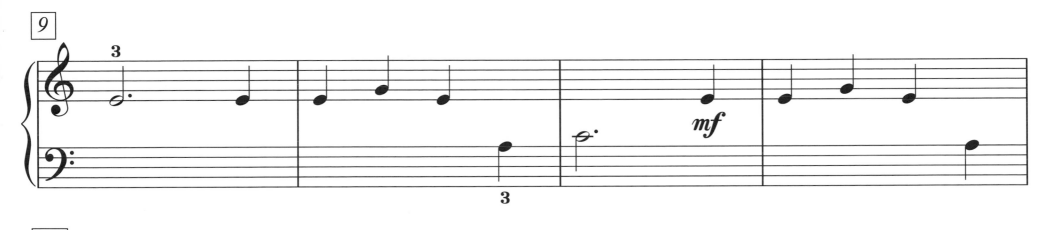

🔍 **Detection Question:** In what measures does the first line come back later in the piece?

London Waltz

JAZZ WALTZ

Flowing and smooth.

Christopher Norton

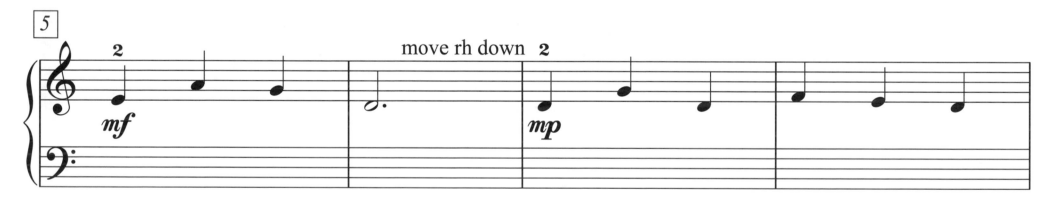

Teacher Duet (student plays one octave higher)

move rh up

Detection Question: How many times does the right hand change position?

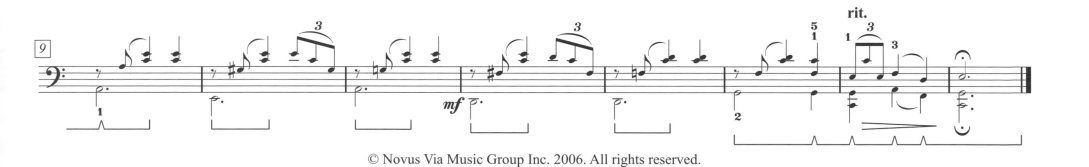

Thinking Of You

LATIN 8-BEAT POP

Listen closely to make sure the tone
of each note is evenly matched.

Christopher Norton

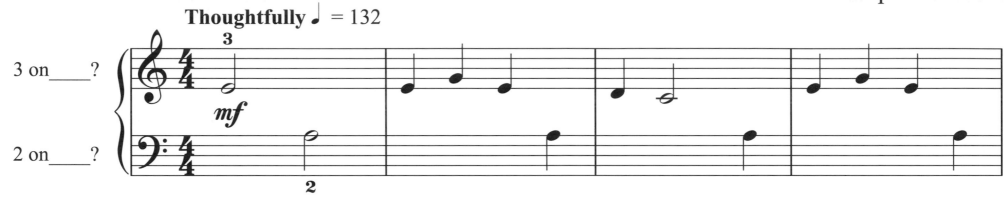

Teacher Duet (student plays one octave higher)

Detection Question: How many times can you find the rhythm ♩ ♩ ♩ in this piece?

Old Timer

COUNTRY WALTZ

Make sure the sound is
gentle and relaxed.

Christopher Norton

_____on C?

_____on G?

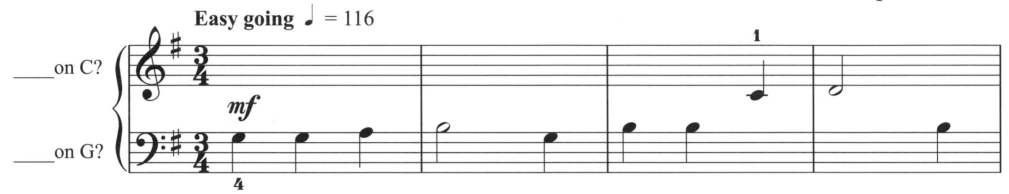

Teacher Duet (student plays one octave higher)

Detection Question: Compare mm. 1-4 with mm. 9-12. What notes are different?

12

Still My Favorite

Smooth and connected.

Christopher Norton

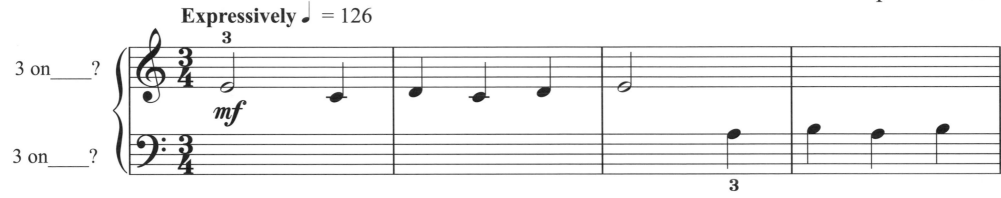

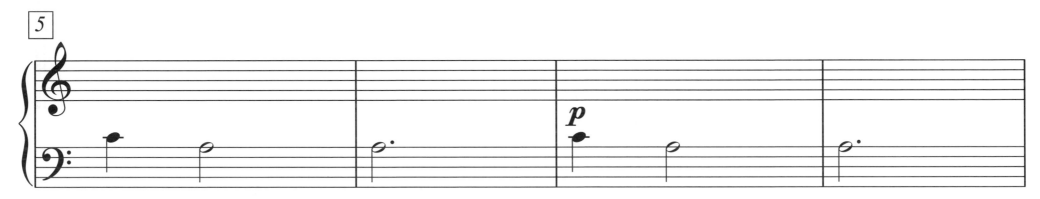

Teacher Duet (student plays one octave higher)

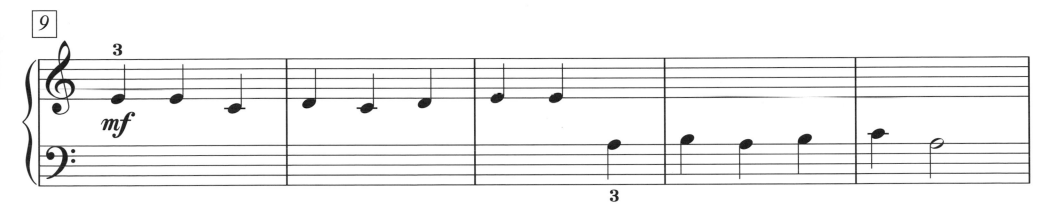

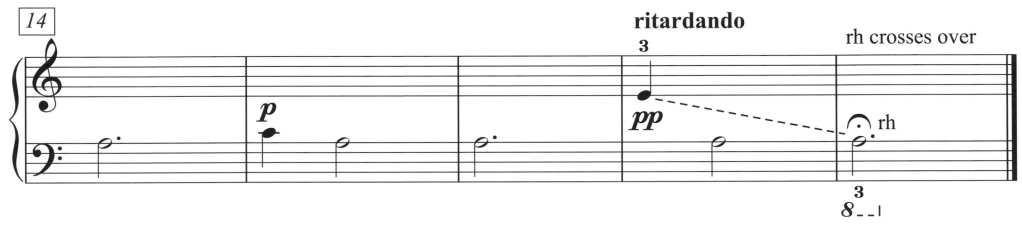

Detection Question: Can you find any echo sections (sections that repeat softly) in this piece? Circle them.

A Little Rhumba

RHUMBA

Light and easy.

Christopher Norton

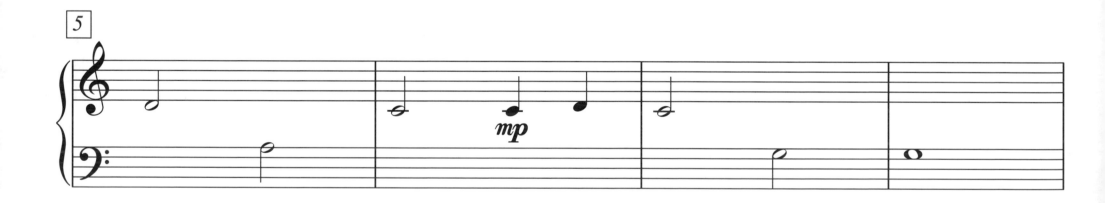

Teacher Duet (student plays one octave higher)

![Detection icon] **Detection Question:** How many intervals of a third can you find in this piece? (Don't forget to check places where the melody changes hands). Circle them.

Calvado

TANGO

This is a piece with a serious mood.

Christopher Norton

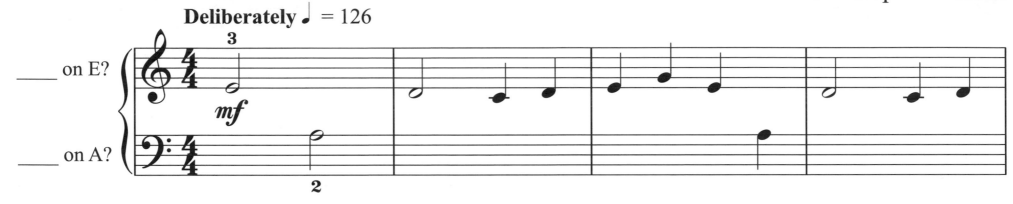

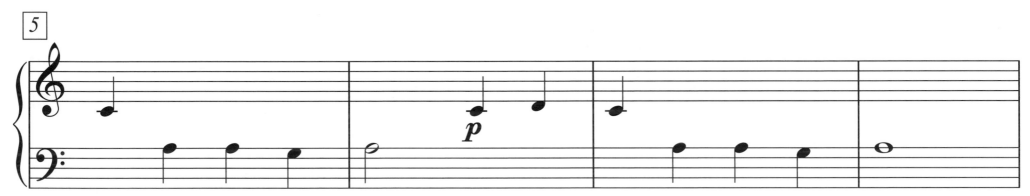

Teacher Duet (student plays one octave higher)

Detection Question: True or False - the left hand only plays two notes in this piece.
What are the names of the left-hand notes?

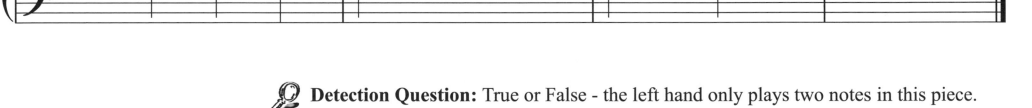

18

Four Square

BIG BAND SWING

Be sure to keep your tempo
very steady.

Christopher Norton

3 on ____?

3 on ____?

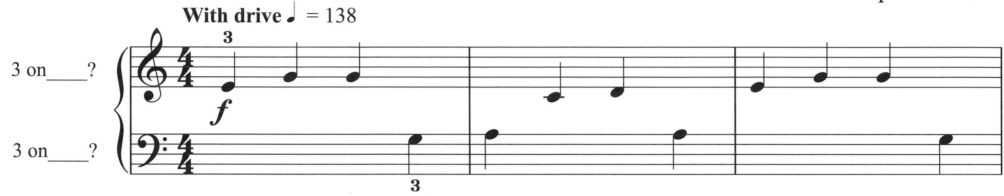

4

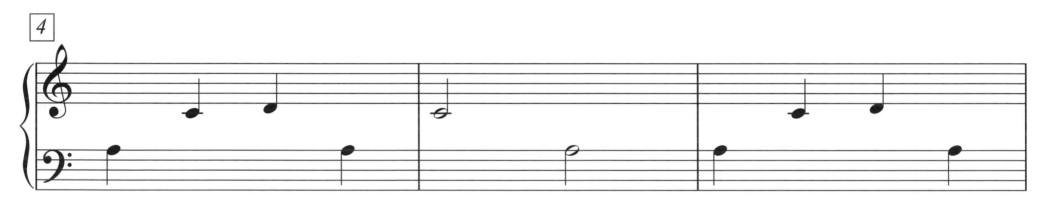

Teacher Duet (student plays one octave higher)

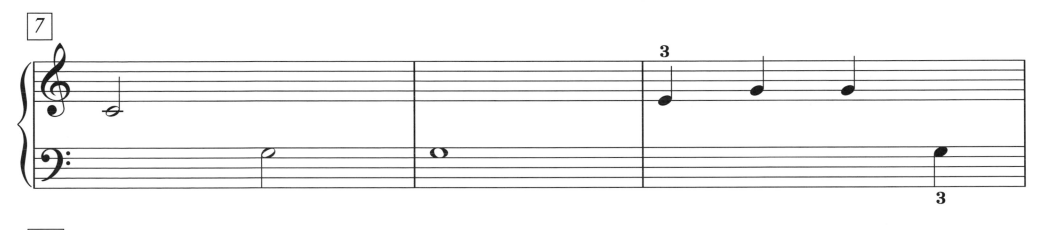

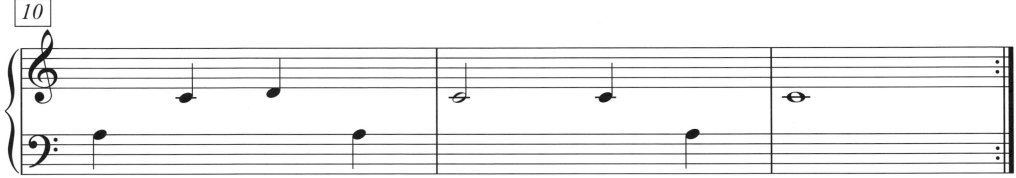

Detection Question: How many half notes (♩) are in this piece?

Green Eyes

COUNTRY SWING

With a gentle sound.

Christopher Norton

on E?

on A?

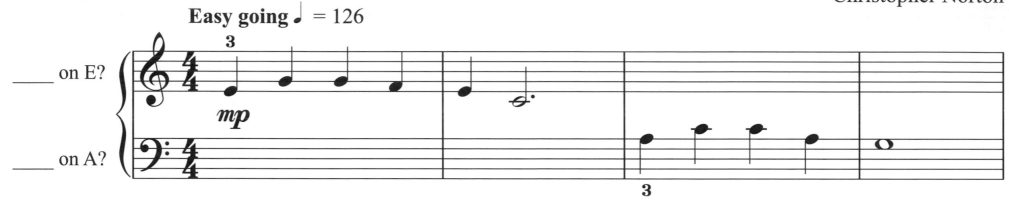

5

Teacher duet (student plays one octave higher)

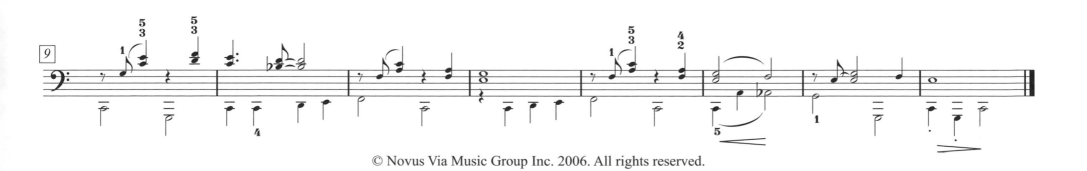

Detection Question: How many measures have the rhythm ♩ 𝅗𝅥 ♩?
Circle them.

June Days

SWING

This piece has an energetic feeling.

Christopher Norton

Brightly ♩ = 138

3 on _____?

3 on _____?

Teacher Duet (student plays one octave higher)

Brightly ♩ = 138

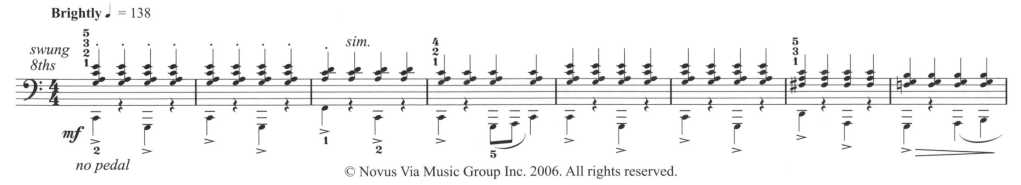

Detection Question: How many different dynamic markings are there in this piece? Circle them. Tell your teacher what they mean.

Still Dreaming

BIG BAND SWING

Smooth and connected.

Christopher Norton

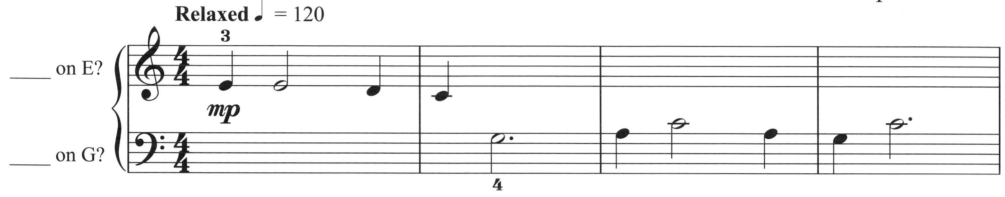

Teacher Duet (student plays one octave higher)

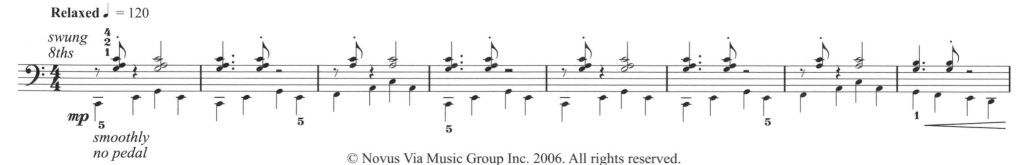

move

rh up

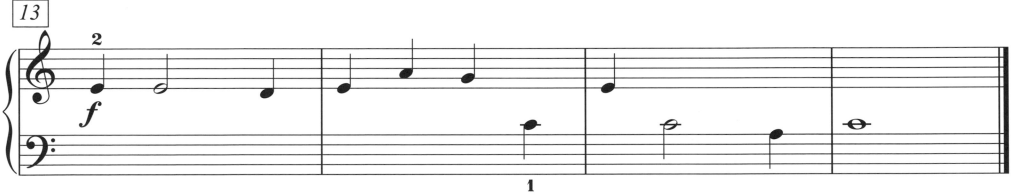

Detection Question: ♩♩ ♩ is a very popular rhythm in pop music.
How many times do you see it in this piece?

Having A Lovely Time

SHUFFLE

Free and easy.

Christopher Norton

Teacher Duet (student plays one octave higher)

Detection Question: What note of the C major pentascale (5-finger position) is missing in the right hand throughout this work?

Not Today

CHA CHA

Be careful not to "punch"
any note.

Christopher Norton

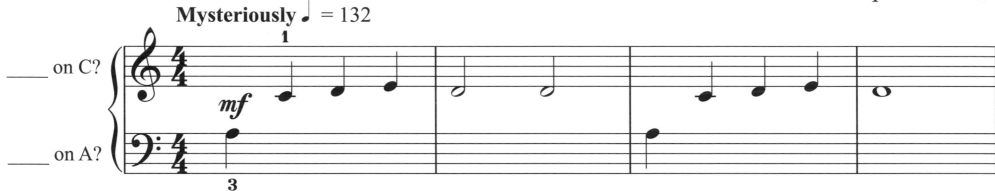

Teacher Duet (student plays one octave higher)

move rh up

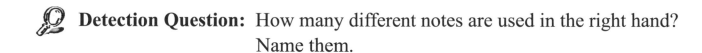

Detection Question: How many different notes are used in the right hand? Name them.

Around The Clock

BOOGIE

A steady tempo is
important in this piece.

Christopher Norton

3 on ____?

2 on ____?

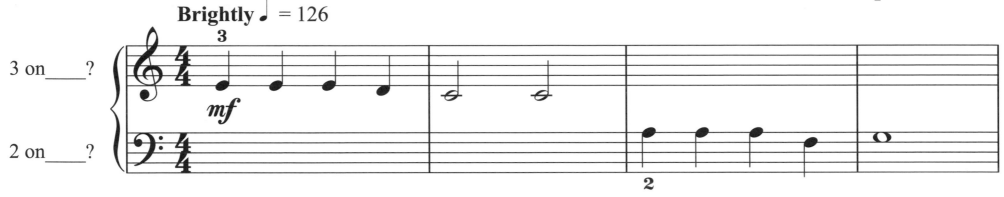

move rh up

Teacher Duet (student plays one octave higher)

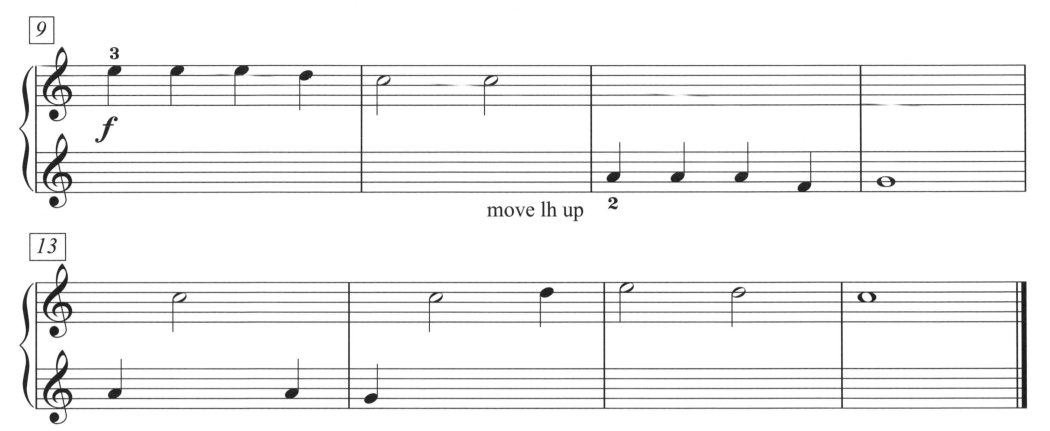

Detection Question: Which one of these note values is missing in this piece?

Circle your answer.

Enchiladas

BOSSA NOVA

Christopher Norton

Be careful not to
"hammer" repeated notes.

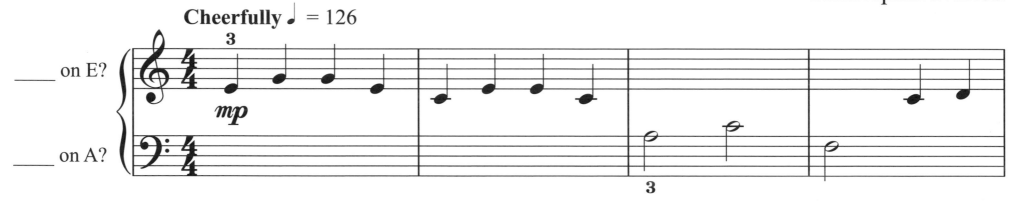

Teacher Duet (student plays one octave higher)

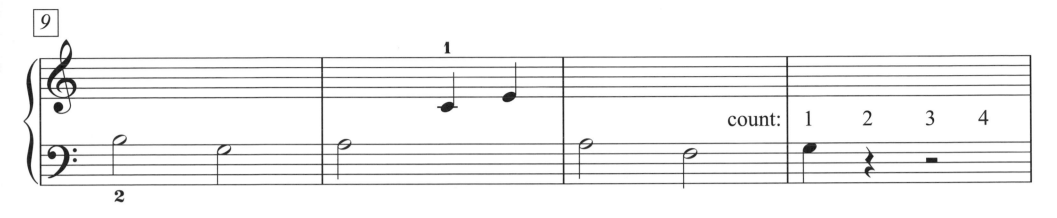

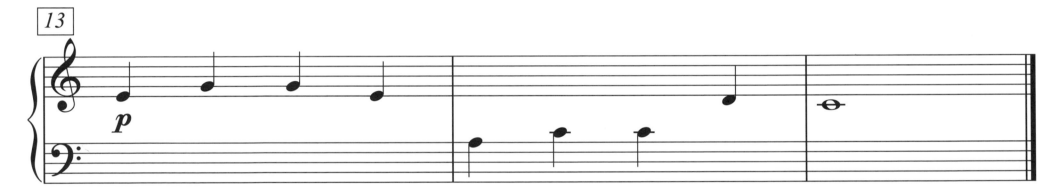

Detection Question: How many measures have this rhythm ♩♩♩♩ in them?

Across The River

SWING

Count carefully when
you play this piece.

Christopher Norton

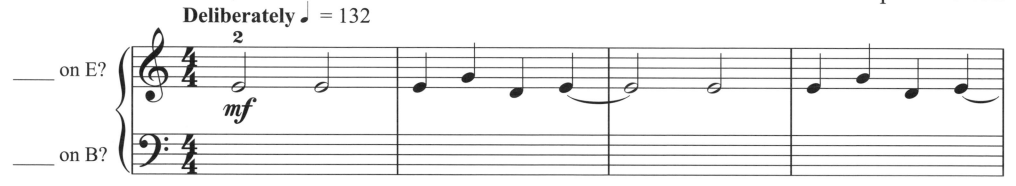

Teacher Duet (student plays one octave higher)

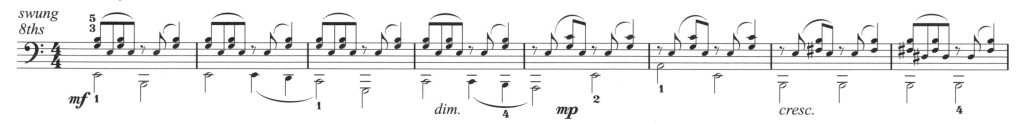

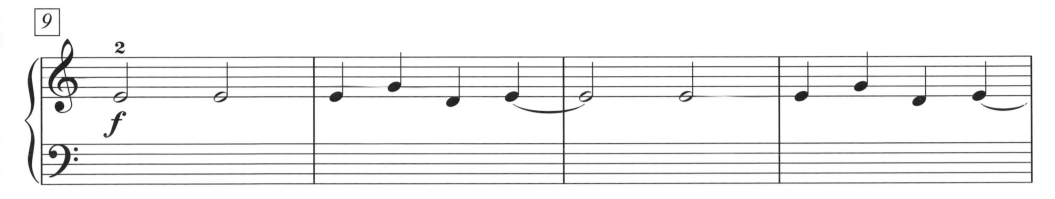

🔍 **Detection Question:** How many ties can you find? Circle them.

Leave Me Alone

Quick and relaxed fingers
are very important here.

CALYPSO

Christopher Norton

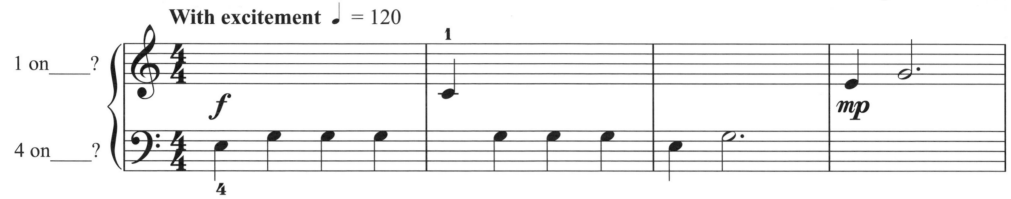

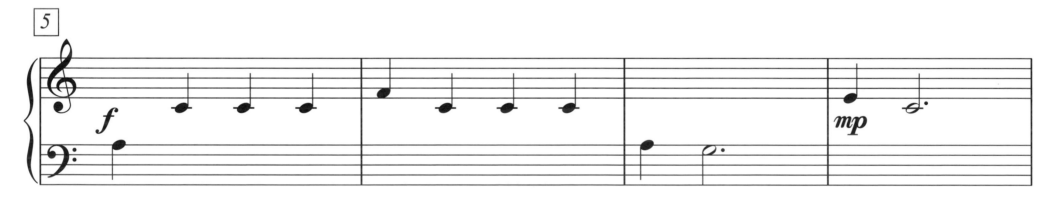

Teacher Duet (student plays one octave higher)

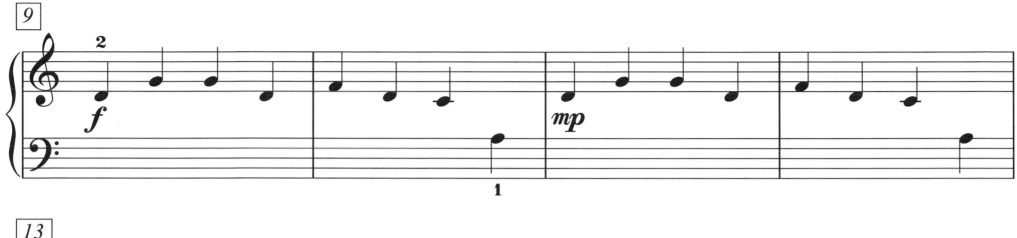

Detection Question: How many times can you find this ♩ ♩. rhythmic pattern? Circle all of them.

LEVEL P REPERTOIRE
Glossary

Symbols

> .... **Accent** emphasize a note or chord. This is often done by playing louder.

𝟴···· .... **All' ottava** "at the octave". If the marking is found above a note or group of notes, play one octave higher. If it is found below a note or group of notes, play one octave lower.

⌒ .... **Fermata** hold the note or rest longer than normal.

f .... **Forte** play loudly.

ff .... **Fortissimo** play very loudly.

▬ .... **Half rest** two beats of silence.

m., mm. .... **Measure, measures** an abbreviation, usually used to give measure numbers.

mf .... **Mezzo forte** play medium loudly.

mp .... **Mezzo piano** play medium softly.

p .... **Piano** play softly.

pp .... **Pianissimo** play very softly.

𝄽 .... **Quarter rest** one beat of silence in 2/4, 3/4, and 4/4 time.

𝄆𝄇 .... **Repeat Sign** play the section of the piece between the two signs again. If there is only one repeat sign (on the right hand side), repeat from the start of the piece.

.... **Tie** connects two next-door notes of the same pitch. The second note is not sounded; its length is added to that of the first note. The same sign is also used to indicate a slur, which you will learn about in Book One.

Terms and Forms

Blues notes ...... A pattern based on a major scale with lowered 3rd, 5th, and 7th notes.

Boogie .... A blues-based piano style (see Blues notes), with continuous 8ths in the left hand part. Examples include: *Around The Clock*

Bossa nova .... A dance style from Brazil, featuring off-beat groupings (2 beats +3 beats +3 beats) in the right hand part of the accompaniment. Examples include: *Enchiladas, The Girl From Ipanema*

Calypso .... A popular song form from the Caribbean island of Trinidad, generally upbeat. Examples include: *Leave Me Alone, Yellow Bird*

Cha cha .... An exciting Latin dance, with a characteristic "cha cha cha" rhythm at the end. Examples include: *Not Today, Never On A Sunday*

Country waltz ... A swing style in 3/4 time (see Swung 8ths) with a strong beat 1 and "oom-pah" accents on beats 2 and 3. Examples include: *Old Timer*

Interval .... The distance from one note to another. To figure out an interval, count the lines and spaces on the staff. The bottom note is counted as "1".

■ Even-numbered intervals (2, 4, 6, 8) are line-space or space-line

■ Odd-numbered intervals (1, 3, 5, 7) are line-line or space-space.

Jazz waltz .... A relaxed swing style in 3/4 time (see Swung 8ths). Examples include: *London Waltz, My Favorite Things*

Latin 8-beat ...... Smooth, medium tempo popular songs with Latin rhythms. Examples
pop   include: *Thinking Of You*

lh .... Play with the left hand.

Motif .... A musical idea.

Off-beat .... An accented note, motif, or phrase played on a normally unaccented beat.

Phrase .... A musical sentence.

rh .... Play with the right hand.

Rhumba .... A dance from South America with syncopated right hand chords played over a steady bass part. Examples include: *A Little Rhumba*

Shuffle .... Based on a style of tap dance where the dancer, wearing soft-soled shoes, "shuffles" their feet in a swung 8ths rhythm. Examples include: *Having A Lovely Time*

Swing .... A fun, dance-like style, usually using swung 8ths.

Swung 8ths ...... 8th notes that are written normally, but played in this gentle dotted rhythm:

Tango............. A rhythmically strict style, with an accent on beat 4. Examples include: *Calvado*

Syncopation ..... Accented notes that briefly change the pattern of accents normally found in a time signature. This word is sometimes used to mean "off-beat".